HIRING AND FIRING

HIRING AND
FIRING

BRIAN TRACY

AMACOM AMERICAN MANAGEMENT ASSOCIATION
New York • Atlanta • Brussels • Chicago • Mexico City
San Francisco • Shanghai • Tokyo • Toronto • Washington, D.C.

Bulk discounts available. For details visit:
www.amacombooks.org/go/specialsales
Or contact special sales:
Phone: 800-250-5308 / E-mail: specialsls@amanet.org
View all the AMACOM titles at: www.amacombooks.org

Library of Congress Cataloging-in-Publication Data

Names: Tracy, Brian, author.
Title: Hiring & firing / Brian Tracy.
Other titles: Hiring and firing.
Description: New York : American Management Association, [2016] | Includes bibliographical references.
Identifiers: LCCN 2016007695 (print) | LCCN 2016014438 (ebook) | ISBN 9780814437513 (hardcover) | ISBN 9780814437520 (ebook)
Subjects: LCSH: Employee selection. | Employees—Recruiting. | Employees—Dismissal of. | Personnel management.
Classification: LCC HF5549.5.S38 T724 2016 (print) | LCC HF5549.5.S38 (ebook) | DDC 658.3/11—dc23
LC record available at http://lccn.loc.gov/2016007695

About AMA

American Management Association (www.amanet.org) is a world leader in talent development, advancing the skills of individuals to drive business success. Our mission is to support the goals of individuals and organizations through a complete range of products and services, including classroom and virtual seminars, webcasts, webinars, podcasts, conferences, corporate and government solutions, business books, and research. AMA's approach to improving performance combines experiential learning—learning through doing—with opportunities for ongoing professional growth at every step of one's career journey.

Printing number
10 9 8 7 6 5 4 3 2 1

CONTENTS

Introduction

HIRING AND FIRING are two of the most important tasks of the manager, the person who is responsible for getting results through others. The first of these tasks is complex and uncertain, and the second is stressful and difficult. Both sets of skills must be learned through study and practice if the manager is to contribute his or her full potential to the organization.

The key executive talent is the ability to recruit, hire, and build a team of effective, competent people. In the modern world, all work is done by teams—by groups of people working together and interacting effectively toward predetermined goals. Therefore, the ability to select team members is critical to the success of the enterprise and to the success of the manager.

The information contained in this book is based on more than 30 years of recruiting, hiring, training, promoting, demoting, and firing men and women at all levels of business. It includes some of the best thinking on the subject by many of the top management experts and executives in the world today. In this book, you will learn methods you can use immediately to improve your hiring and firing abilities, to enhance productivity, to increase performance and profits, and to bring about higher levels of cooperation, teamwork, and harmony in your office or workplace.

Because individual human beings are so complex and unpredictable, even the best hiring skills will give you a success rate of only about 66 percent. One-third of the people you hire will probably not work out in the long run, according to the best statistics available on the subject. However, you can greatly increase the odds in your favor by following the recommendations in this book.

The Flipside of Hiring

I started my career in business at the age of twelve, mowing lawns. I bought a lawnmower and went from house to house soliciting work and cutting the grass. I hired my first employee when I was thirteen. He was my best friend. I also fired my first employee at the age of thirteen—no longer my best friend.

Through the years I have hired hundreds of people. I've also fired hundreds of people over the course of my career, not all of them people who I had hired personally—I inherited some of them when I stepped into management positions.

Over time, I read the very best material I could find on the subjects of hiring and firing, and I continue to keep up to date on these subjects. I have taken graduate courses on personnel selection, attended talks, listened to audio programs, read an enormous number of books and articles, and studied, analyzed, and given a great deal of thought to hiring and firing.

What I am going to teach you in the pages ahead are twenty-one key ideas you can use to hire the best people, to help ensure their success, and if necessary, to fire people who do not work out well within your organization.

What you will learn are simple, proven methods and techniques that you can use for the rest of your career. Let's get started.

ONE

The Selection Process

THE SELECTION process is the key to your success as an executive and to the success of your company. The first law of management is selection. Ninety-five percent of the success of any enterprise is determined by the people chosen to work in the enterprise.

If you select in haste, you will repent at leisure. Most hasty hiring decisions lead to sorrow later. A hiring decision involves not only your life and your activities, but also the life, complexities, attitudes, personality, skills, and involvement of another human being. It involves people in areas that affects their lives as much as anything else, other than their families. When you have to hire, therefore, the best rule is to hire slowly and to select carefully.

Take Your Time

Hiring is an art. It cannot be hurried. It is like painting a portrait or preparing a gourmet meal. Occasionally you can do it quickly, but in most cases you have to take your time to be sure to make the right decision.

When you are in the position of hiring someone, it is common to make the mistake of hiring as a solution to a problem. You are overloaded with work. You have a hole, a job that needs to be done because somebody has quit or the company is expanding.

You therefore look upon hiring a person as a solution to this problem. You then go into the marketplace, grab someone, and throw that person at the problem. You hope that the new hire will somehow plug up the hole.

This is the worst of all approaches. Many entrepreneurs or people starting and running small and medium-size businesses make this mistake of looking at people as solutions to problems. This is absolutely the wrong attitude and approach to the business of hiring.

Poor Selection Is Expensive

Poor selection is very expensive. Don't ever think that if it doesn't work out, you will just fire the person and get someone else. This is the attitude of a manager who is inexperienced or incompetent and who should not be in the position of hiring people in the first place.

Hiring is expensive for three reasons. Number one is that you lose your time—the time that it takes you to go through the selection process, prepare, interview, hire, and train the new individual.

Second, you lose the amount of money that you spent in salaries or wages, benefits, and training on your new hire, because everything learned is lost to the company when the person is fired and departs.

The third thing you lose is that individual's productivity, plus the productivity in between the firing and when the next person comes on board.

In addition, firing is expensive in terms of morale. In any company where a lot of firing goes on and there is high turnover of staff, you invariably have low morale, low performance, and low productivity because everybody is continually wondering if they are going to be next.

According to the personnel experts, it costs between three and six times the individual's annual salary to hire someone and then lose them when they don't work out. These are just the actual financial costs. This is why companies that have high rates of turnover are almost invariably low profit companies. The companies that are the most profitable have turnover rates that are as low as 1 percent or 2 percent per year.

Even if you are in a hurry to find the right person and get someone into that job, practice what Shakespeare said: "Make haste slowly."

ACTION EXERCISES

1. Think of the best hire you ever made. Who was it and how did you go about making your decision?

2. Think about the worst hire you ever made. What mistakes did you make? What did you learn?

TWO

Think Through the Job

THOMAS J. WATSON, founder of IBM, had signs throughout the IBM offices, on every wall, with the single word "THINK!" Each person in the company was encouraged to look at those signs continually whenever making decisions or solving problems.

This lesson applies to hiring as well. Nothing could be more important than your ability to think through the job in the first place. Think through the actual requirements of the job. What will the person have to do, day in and day out? What specific results do you expect this person to achieve?

Stop and Think

When you decide to hire a new person, step back mentally and pause for a while. Don't fall into the trap of automatically hiring people who are just like the people they are replacing. Take the time to analyze the current responsibilities of the position, as if you were starting anew.

Imagine a factory. A factory has three processes. The first is the *inputs*: the money, time, resources, raw materials, management, and so on that the company needs to operate.

The second process is the *activities* that the factory engages in to produce the products that are to be sold in the marketplace. In the factory, production activities take place and, as a result, outputs occur.

The third process is the production of specific *outputs* that can be used by others and combined with other work or activities to create a product or service that can be sold in the marketplace.

Each Person as a Factory

Think of each individual as a factory as well. The individual has inputs—the knowledge, skills, talents, background, and experiences that individual brings to the job. While working, the individual performs a series of functions, tasks, and activities that constitute the real work of the employee.

Finally, the employee is expected to produce specific, measurable outputs, the accomplishment of which will determine the employee's success at the job.

When thinking through the job, ask yourself, "Exactly what specific, measurable outputs do I want from this new person, and what skills will this person need in order to accomplish these required outputs?"

Update Your Thinking

In times of turbulence and rapid change such as today, and for the indefinite future, the position you are hiring for now will probably require new or different skills from those you have needed before, or from those that a previous employee was hired for. Very often, the job has changed and evolved over time. What you might need is not a replacement for a departing employee but a completely different person altogether.

What *qualities* does the person need to have to perform the job and get the desired results? You don't need a superman or superwoman for a job that requires only average competence and intelligence and which leads to the production of ordinary products and services. You do not need a superstar to do an average job that is not particularly challenging or demanding.

On the other hand, if you have an extremely challenging and demanding job, you will need to hire a very skilled person. Be realistic with regard to the qualities and skills you require to do this particular job because you're going to have to pay for them.

Is the Job Doable?

In thinking through the job, Peter Drucker suggests that you ask, "Is the job doable?" In other words, is the job that you are trying to hire for a job that can be done by one normal person?

Very often, jobs cannot be done by a single person. They are too complex, or they require conflicting skill sets or temperaments. The job you are designing may require that a person do two different things that conflict, or the job may just be too big for one person.

Some years ago, I initiated the importation and distribution of a line of Japanese vehicles into the country. In the first year, we set up sixty-four dealerships to sell and service these vehicles. This required a super salesman, which we had. But we also insisted that he work with the finance department, parts department, services department, and sales department of each new dealership, and complete large amounts of paperwork that were essential to the smooth functioning of the sale of our cars through these dealerships.

Divide the Tasks

The sales executive we had was excellent at convincing dealers to carry our line of automobiles. But he was terrible with paperwork. This became a bone of continuous contention. We were always frustrated and arguing over delays and incomplete documents that other people in our distribution network required in order to do their jobs properly.

I finally had a revelation. Great salespeople are not necessarily great with paperwork or details. But our service manager loved to do detail work. His temperament was exactly suited for filling out every line and blank in our application forms for vehicles, parts, service, and financing.

Our solution was to focus our top salesman on building relationships and opening up new dealerships—the key to our financial success. After the dealership had been appointed, our service manager would go in to make sure that all the paperwork was completed in a timely and accurate fashion. Result? No more problems.

Make sure that the job you are hiring for can be done by a single person. Be prepared to change the description of the job on a regular basis as you get more experience and more information about the job and what actually needs to be done.

ACTION EXERCISES

1. Think about a job that needs to done or a position that needs to be filled in your company. Exactly what results will be expected of the person in that job?

2. Identify the three most important skills and the past experiences that a person will need to do this job in an excellent fashion.

THREE

Writing the Job Description

THERE IS A saying in business: "Before you do anything, you have to do something else first." Before you even think of hiring someone, you have to write out the job description in detail.

Clarity is your best friend. The more clarity you have with regard to exactly the person you want to hire, the easier it will be for you to make an excellent decision later.

Think on paper. Start creating your job description by standing back and thinking through what the individual will be doing from the time work starts in the morning until finishing time in the evening.

List every task, function, and responsibility that the new person will have. Write it out like a checklist, as if you were describing the job to the kind of person you expect to do it, step by step. This really forces you to think about the job with much greater clarity. This task takes work, which is why most people don't do it. But because they are unclear about exactly what the new person will be expected to do, many managers make mistake after mistake, hiring the wrong person again and again.

Make a List

Once you have written out your list, go through the items and set priorities for each. This is quite simple. Next to each of the items on your list you write "very important," "important," and "not so important."

If you like, you can list them as 1, 2, or 3 in importance. Or you can use the ABC method of prioritizing the work functions, with "A" being very important, "B" being important, and "C" being not so important. You can then organize them further as A-1, A-2, and A-3 tasks or responsibilities.

You must be especially clear about what is "very important," because these are the tasks that you must be sure that the candidate can do in an excellent fashion during your interview process.

Another way that you can organize your list to achieve better clarity for yourself and others is to take 100 points and divide them up among the items on your list. Some items will receive a high number of points and others a low number of points, or no points at all.

When you allocate points across the list of tasks, functions, and responsibilities that you desire in the candidate, the highest number of points will go to previous proven experience in getting the results that are most important to success in this job.

Musts vs. Likes

When you are hiring a person, you will have "musts" and "likes." The difference between the two is that the candidate *must* be capable of performing the "musts." The "likes" are simply preferences that are not essential to job performance.

Some of the "musts" are the person's proven ability to do the most important parts of the job in an excellent fashion. Some of the "likes" may be "lives close to the office," or "engages in physical fitness activities."

Another example of a "must" might be "nonsmoker." Once I hired a woman who lied about this habit. I asked her why she smelled of tobacco smoke and she said it was because her boyfriend was a heavy smoker. Later, I found her closing her office door so that she could smoke. Eventually, her office smelled like a tobacco barn. We had to let her go.

Look for a Good Personality

Think about the people your new hire will be working with. Coworkers will have a major impact on whether the new person will be successful at the job. Will your new hire be compatible with these coworkers?

In our company, we introduce each new candidate who

has passed the initial screening to each of the people he or she will be working with. The other members of the staff perform mini-interviews with the prospective employee, which they share later with everyone who will be involved in the final decision. We never hire anyone who the prospective coworkers do not like.

Look for Fit

What sort of personality and attitude will a person need for this type of job? The number-one reason people do not work out at jobs is because they fail to "fit." Their personalities and temperaments are not consistent with the way the companies operate.

For example, if you are hiring for an internal job for clerical, accounting, or computer work, a person who has a self-contained or quiet personality will be your best choice. If you are hiring for a sales, marketing, or customer-oriented job, you will be seeking a person who is more outgoing and extroverted.

We have discovered that people who, in person, may be a bit shy and reserved often turn out to be dynamic when they are on the phone in customer relations positions, displaying warm, high-energy personalities that make them personable and persuasive.

Finally, remember when you are writing the job description that there is a difference between what a person can do and what a person will do. Especially in sales and marketing, we have learned that there are many people who have the ability to make sales, but they won't go out and make sales because of high levels of call reluctance or fear of rejection.

The more time that you spend thinking through and writing down every detail of the description of the candidate that you want, the more likely you are to find and recognize that person in the hiring process. Make haste slowly.

ACTION EXERCISES

1. Identify the two best qualities of your best-performing people. What do they have in common?

2. What are the two most important skills you look for in a new hire?

FOUR

Finding Suitable Candidates

AN IMPORTANT part of the selection process is for you to generate a sufficient number of suitable candidates from which to choose. If you are hiring for an important job, you will have to attract a large number of resumes at the beginning to be sure that you get the right person at the end.

Cast a Wide Net

In his book *Double Double*, Cameron Herold estimates that it takes him 16 candidates, on average, to find one person worthy of being hired. Other executives have found that they require 250 job applications to get as many as 16 people to interview, out of which will come the one person that they hire.

The rule in finding suitable candidates is to cast a wide net. Remember that the best people for your company are probably already working somewhere else and are either unhappy or underpaid, or both. One of your chief responsibilities as a manager is to be constantly on the lookout for people who are already working and to offer them much better positions.

Start Internally

If you are part of a small company and are growing, recruiting new people is a major job responsibility for you. Sales managers, for example, should be spending 20 percent of their time, or the equivalent of one full day a week, identifying, interviewing, and recruiting new and better salespeople.

If your company is larger, recruiting starts with your human resources or personnel department. Start by conducting an internal search for a new candidate. Write out the job description and circulate it so that everyone in your company knows that you are looking for a particular type of person.

Companies that hire from the inside have the lowest turnover rates and the highest levels of productivity.

One company I worked with hired almost entirely either from within, or as a result of staff recommendations. They would offer a $1,500 bonus to any of their employees who brought them a new person. They would pay $500 when the new person was hired, $500 more if the new person stayed for six months, and the third $500 if the person stayed for a year.

As a result of this bonus system, everyone in the company was continually looking for people they could recommend. An advantage of this system is that no one wanted to recommend someone who would reflect badly on him or her personally. The candidates who they recommended were almost invariably vetted in advance by the people referring them in the first place.

Use the Internet

The Internet is probably the most important source of job openings and potential employees, at all levels. Almost anyone that you could possibly desire to hire as an employee is on Facebook, LinkedIn, Craigslist, Monster, or CareerBuilder. It is amazing what you can find if you simply use Google and type in the position or title of the person you are seeking. There are said to be as many as 2,000 small and larger sites where potential job applicants register to make themselves known.

In our company, and in most companies today, the initial application process is online. Prospective applicants are directed to a website and asked to fill out an application with the answers to several specific questions related to the job. This is an excellent way to screen a lot of candidates quickly since most of the people who apply will not be suitable and can be quickly winnowed out.

Another way that many companies recruit is by communicating with their personal contacts. They send out e-mail descriptions to everyone in their database who is in a position to recommend prospective candidates. In my research for my Creative Job Search program, I found that as many as 85 percent of important jobs are filled by referrals and recommendations and are never advertised.

Use the Professionals

For specialized and executive positions, you can use the services of a professional headhunter. These experts can save you an enormous amount of time because of their contacts, experience, and particular expertise in finding the right people for specific jobs. They normally charge 15 percent to 25 percent of the first year's salary as a commission, but they are usually worth it.

What's Wrong?

If you are having trouble finding enough candidates for the job you are advertising, there are usually one of two problems. Either the job you are describing cannot be done by a single person or the money that you are offering is not acceptable to a person with the talent to do the job you are hiring for.

If you are offering an attractive job, with a sufficient salary, working for a company where there is opportunity for growth and advancement, you should be able to attract an endless supply of good candidates. If not, think about revisiting the job description to make it more attractive and doable.

ACTION EXERCISES

1. Identify the sources of your best employees to date. Where did they come from?

2. Identify two additional ways that you could attract candidates and give each of them a try right away.

FIVE

The Interviewing Process

YOUR INTERVIEWING process should be carefully thought through and designed for maximum efficiency. Many companies today have systems in place to attract applications, invite the applicants to group interviews, do one-on-one interviews with acceptable candidates, give them tests, check their references, make them offers, and set up their training and orientation schedules.

Plan in Advance
Once you have decided, based on the online or other form of application, that you want to interview a job candidate with a view to hiring that person, you must plan the interviewing process and the interviewing sequence in advance, before you meet the individual.

Most managers either talk too much, or talk too little, or ask simple questions based on the information in the person's application. They have never been trained in the interviewing process—even though it is one of the most critical things you must do as a manager in your entire career.

Over the years, I have developed a method or process of interviewing that I have taught to thousands of managers. Many of them have come back to me and said that this process had a major positive impact on their careers.

Follow Your Plan

First of all, write out and follow a logical questioning sequence for the interview. Don't attempt to wing it.

When you first meet the candidate, sit him or her down, introduce yourself, and then put the person at ease. The job interview is one of the most stressful events that an individual goes through. Your job is to reduce this stress before you begin.

My method is to start off by saying, "Please relax. We are not going to make any final decision today, in any case. Let us deal with this interview objectively, as the lawyers say, 'Without prejudice.'"

Then I'll continue: "This means that I will tell you about the job and what the company does. You tell me what you do and what you are thinking and feeling about the job, and we'll work together to see if there is a fit. You want to be happy with this position, and we want to be happy with whoever does this job. If this interview process doesn't work out, it won't be a reflection on either one of us. So just relax."

Then you explain what the company does, what the job requires, and what kind of person you're looking for. What you are trying to do is to objectify the job. You are trying to refer to the job as if it was out there on the table between you, and you are having a discussion about it.

Ask a Lot of Questions

You then go through the highlights of the candidate's resume and begin asking questions that expand on the candidate's background and history. You apply the 80/20 rule. You ask questions and listen 20 percent of the time while you encourage the candidate to answer and speak 80 percent of the time. Whatever you do, avoid dominating the conversation.

There is a powerful question to encourage people to open up with you. After you tell them something about the responsibilities of the job you ask, "How do you feel about that?"

Everyone has feelings. They are neither positive nor negative. When you ask someone "How do you feel about that?" the candidate will often reply with extensive answers that give you opportunities to learn more and more, which will help you to make a good decision.

In a job interview, you are looking for a person who can get the results that you have identified earlier. This means that you are continually asking questions about what the person has done in the past relative to the most important outputs of this job, and how it worked out. What were the person's successes and failures, and what does the person think and feel about them?

One of the best indicators of success in life is creativity. And one of the best indicators of creativity is *curiosity*. A good job candidate wants to interview you and learn more about you and the company.

The more questions that a candidate asks, the more likely it is that he or she is a qualified person. The best people available are those who interview companies to decide where to work, rather than going around being interviewed and having their careers determined by people selecting them for positions.

Look for a Hard Worker

The most important quality for success in life is a willingness to work hard. Ask them how they feel about working late on occasion or on weekends or holidays if that is necessary to get the job done.

If they express any reluctance about working evenings and weekends to do the job, you can be sure they are going to be average "nine-to-fivers" if you hire them.

Successful candidates are goal-oriented. They see jobs as opportunities to help them achieve their personal goals by helping companies achieve their business goals. The best candidates of all have clear, written goals and plans to achieve them, of which this potential job is a part of that plan.

Look for a Sense of Urgency

A sense of urgency is a key quality of the best people, both employees and managers. John Swan, a personnel recruiter and headhunter, developed what he called the SWAN formula. In this case, the word SWAN stands for "Smart, Works hard, Ambitious, and Nice."

Look for someone who is ambitious and just a little bit hungry. You want someone who is eager to start and sees the job as a springboard to a better life and who will tell you something like, "I really want to work here rather than anywhere else."

If you interview someone and are thinking of hiring him or her, you ask, "When would you be prepared to start if we were to offer you the job?" The very best person wants to start immediately. A person who wants to take a rest or a break before starting the job is not the kind of person you want to drive your organization forward.

Interviewing and hiring the right people is a key skill of management. Fortunately, it is a skill set that you can learn with study and practice. The better you become at interviewing, the more valuable the contribution you will make to your company, sometimes for years into the future.

ACTION EXERCISES

1. Make a list of the key questions you want to ask each job candidate to test whether this person is right for your company.

2. Base your hiring criteria on the SWAN formula, looking for candidates who are smart, work hard, show ambition, and are nice.

SIX

Use the Law of Three

THE KEY TO the excellent interviewing process is what I call the Law of Three. This law says that you should look at a minimum of three good candidates, interview the one you like best a minimum of three times, and interview that person in at least three different settings or locations.

When you are interviewing for any job, always speak to a minimum of three people. Don't get stuck on the very first one, no matter how good that candidate appears at that initial interview.

One of my rules is that "job candidates will never look better in their lives than on the first interview."

It is at the first interview that the candidate will impress you the most. If for some reason he does not impress you at the first meeting, he is not going to impress you later on.

If you really like the candidate, interview the person three times: first in your office, second down the hall in another space or over a coffee, and third out of the office over lunch. I have found that very often people who look terrific in the first interview may start to fade in the second interview, and by the third time you interview them you realize they are totally inappropriate.

A fourth application of the Law of Three is to have the job candidate interviewed by at least three other people. When I was a young business owner, I would meet a person and hire on the spot, if I liked the person. As a result, I made a lot of hiring mistakes that cost me an enormous amount of time, trouble, money, and even lawsuits. Then I decided not to rely on my own judgments. Instead, if I liked a person, I would introduce the person to another member of my staff in the next office and leave the two of them together to talk about the job, the business, and whatever other subjects came up.

My staff member would be aware of this process and, after a few minutes, take the person to the next office to chat someone else. Often, job candidates were interviewed by six or seven people in the office before they were thanked for their time and told that we would get in touch with them later.

Take Your Time Interviewing

Hewlett-Packard (HP) was famous for its "seven-part interview process." Managers interviewed each candidate a minimum of seven times. Four different line managers interviewed the candidate; they represented the level of manager that this person would be working under. At the end of the process, after both individual and group interviews, these four managers came together and voted. The vote had to be unanimous. If one of the four managers was uncomfortable with the candidate, that person was passed over for the job.

The reason the company was so careful about the interview process was because it planned to hire people for life. Because of this philosophy, the turnover rates at Hewlett-Packard were some of the lowest in the high-tech industry for many years. (In 2015, HP announced a total of 84,000 layoffs due to dramatically changing market conditions.)

Lower Your Turnover Rate

One of the top management consulting firms in New York has a process of hiring that includes a minimum of twenty-five interviews. As a result, the firm makes excellent hires. Its turnover rate is almost zero percent. The senior executives of the firm are involved in every final interview, even for a receptionist position. Because they are so careful about selection, they have people who have stayed with the firm for twenty, thirty, and forty years.

Nothing sorts out candidates better than a multiple interview process. If you don't use a multiple interview process, you're going to end up with people who were turned away by another company that more carefully screens employees using multiple interviews.

After the multiple interviews, bring everyone together to discuss the candidate. Often, people I thought looked very good turned out to be terrible choices. On one occasion, I almost hired a senior manager for a key job. But when the members of my staff had a chance to talk with him, they came back to me and were unanimously opposed to him having anything to do with our company.

Never rely solely on your own judgment. Involve as many other people as possible in the interviewing process. Have the person interviewed by at least three others whose opinions you respect.

The Group Interview Process

Southwest Airlines is famous for its group interview process. The company invites a group of applicants to a meeting where the interviewer in charge asks the candidates a series of questions. These questions can be quite innocuous, such as:

"What is your favorite movie, and why?"

"Why do you want to work for this company?"

"What do you have to offer that would make you a good choice for this company?"

"What has been your most important experience in life, and how did it affect you?"

The purpose of this process is to get the candidates both talking and listening to the others. What the recruiters are looking for is not whether the answers are good or bad, but how the prospective candidates interact with each other. Do they smile, listen, applaud, and encourage the others when they are answering these questions, or do they just sit there waiting for their turn?

Southwest makes its final decision based on the interactive skills of the candidates, not the answers. It is a system that works very well for the company. What system do you use?

ACTION EXERCISES

1. Plan out how to use the Law of Three the next time you hire someone, and follow your plan.

2. Consider interviewing candidates in groups to see how they interact with each other.

SEVEN

Past Performance as the Best Predictor

PAST PERFORMANCE in previous jobs is the best indicator of what the candidate is likely to do in the future. Performance is everything. As Henry Ford said, "You can't build a reputation on what you are going to do."

You should resolve to hire based on proven past performance only. It is not how good the person looks or how much you like someone, nor the person's wonderful personality. All that matters is what the individual has done in the past.

Unless you hire green recruits from college or university and train them from the ground up, the only way that you can hire intelligently is by looking at what people have done in previous jobs. This means that you have to be very careful in checking up on the backgrounds of your candidates to make sure that their claimed past performance is consistent with the truth. Most people exaggerate their performance tremendously on resumes and in interviews. They are not dishonest, but they usually claim credit for results that they were only partially responsible for achieving.

Look for Achievement Orientation

David McClelland, the Harvard psychologist and author of *The Achieving Society*, found that people are motivated to perform by one of three types of personal drives.

The first is the need for *individual* accomplishment. This is the person who derives his greatest sense of accomplishment and personal worth from achieving something by himself. These people make excellent salespeople and managers and like to engage in any activity where they are totally responsible for the end result.

The second type of person is someone who enjoys being a part of a *team*, working well and cooperating with others. Their greatest sense of achievement is participating in something that their team or workforce accomplished by working together over an extended period of time.

The third type is the individual who enjoys organizing, coordinating, and motivating a group of people to accomplish a task. This person makes the ideal supervisor, manager, or *leader* motivated to do everything possible to get results through other people.

Interview for Achievement

When you interview candidates, ask about what achievements were most responsible for their greatest sense of personal pride and satisfaction. They will usually give you achievements based on one of the three types of motivation. This will give you an idea of the kind of job for which this person would be appropriate or even ideal.

If someone's greatest achievement was growing a garden or finishing *War and Peace* or something that did not require a lot of sustained effort or persistence, then you will find that these qualities do not translate well to challenging jobs that require a lot of focus and determination, but might be ideal for administrative work. You may, however, be looking for a person whose greatest achievement was doubling sales, breaking a record, driving profitability to a new high, winning a contest, or achieving a medal or award of some kind. Interview for this type of background.

The Past Predicts the Future

In psychology, we know that previous achievement lays down a mental template in the individual. After a person has achieved something worthwhile, nothing will satisfy him but to achieve something even greater in the future. People with past histories of achievement will strive to duplicate that performance working for you if you give them the opportunity.

Ask candidates what experience they have that they think qualifies them to do the job that you have explained. Ask them what they think they are going to be able to do to achieve success in this job. What special qualities or abilities do they have?

My friend, Chet Holmes, was a top sales manager and often recruited salespeople into his company. After he had interviewed a person for a short period of time, he would say something like: "I don't hear the sound of a winner or a top achiever when I talk to you."

This was a test question. He waited to see how the individual would respond. Some people would just say, "Okay, if that's the way you feel . . ." and leave the interview, discouraged.

On the other hand, some candidates would become irate and challenge him for having the audacity to suggest that they were not winners in the past and potential winners in the future. These were the people he hired, not the people who gave up at the first sign of rejection.

Always look for a candidate with the experience that directly links into the results that you want the person in this job to accomplish. Check her track record carefully and grill her on what she's done in the past. Avoid bringing in a new or inexperienced person for a new job. This is high-risk strategy for any but the largest and richest firms.

Especially if you are the owner of a small or medium-sized business, you should only hire people who have work experience that thoroughly qualifies them to get the results that you want, almost from the day they start work.

ACTION EXERCISES

1. List three types of previous success experiences that would most likely predict success in your company.

2. List two ways to determine if a job candidate is a hard worker.

EIGHT

Checking Resumes and References

CHECKING RESUMES and references is an essential part of the hiring process. From experience, employers have discovered that resumes are usually inaccurate, sometimes professionally produced, and often dishonest or misleading.

In more than 50 percent of cases, individuals will overstate their qualifications in some way. We have also discovered that referrals or reference letters are not worth very much because often they are handed out in exchange for the person leaving in peace: "If you accept our severance offer and depart without making any trouble, we will write you a nice letter of reference for your next employer, and we will only say nice things if anyone calls us to ask about you."

Check Resumes Personally

Checking referrals and the background of each candidate is a vital function performed by placement agencies, if you use one. But, like a detective, you must check at least three different referrals to find out the truth about the candidate before you hire anyone.

One of the best ways to get information on a candidate is to quickly go onto Facebook, LinkedIn, and Twitter to look at his profile and the kind of messages he sends and receives. This can be quite revealing.

The more important the candidate and the job, the more important it is for you to check referrals personally. Phone and speak directly to the person who gave the referral. Recognize that very often, the person you are contacting is not going to give you a bad reference or you would not have been given her information in the first place.

How to Check References

Call the person you were referred to, introduce yourself, and explain that you are interviewing John Smith for this or that particular position. Then ask if you can ask a couple of questions about John because he's given this person as a reference. Let the reference know that you are asking for help and promise confidentiality.

Then, ask the reference to tell you about John's primary strengths, especially as they might apply to the job you are interviewing him for. This requires a positive answer. Very often, the person you are calling will say, "Well, he's good at this and good at that."

Then you ask the person to tell you about some of the weaknesses that the candidate had demonstrated in his previous job. Many companies are very cautious about talking about the weaknesses of past employees, but often they'll say something like, "John lacks drive," or "John could use his time more efficiently."

The Best Question

Perhaps the most revealing question that you can ask a reference is this: "Would you hire this person back again?"

Sometimes, the individual will react in a positive way and say, "If we were not going through this transition, we would hire John back in a minute." This is a very good thing to hear.

On the other hand, sometimes the previous employer will answer spontaneously, "Never. Not on your life!"

This is a great question that cuts right to the core of the issue.

The Final Question

Before you hang up, ask the reference this final question: "Is there anything else I should know?"

One of the rules of conversation or negotiation is that the most important information comes out in the last 20 percent of the conversation. The first part of the conversation can therefore be general. Once you have established some rapport with the referral, this person will feel an affinity with you as a fellow manager and fellow employer.

You are a boss and he is a boss. You are hiring and firing as part of your job, and so is he. The two of you have a lot in common.

When you ask the final question—"Is there anything else I should know?"—the person will often say, "Well, there is one thing you should be aware of."

The Critical Factor

What they tell you at this point may well be the critical factor. Some years ago I was hiring a senior manager to act as the liaison with my national chain of distributors in the field. She was extremely personable, charming, and full of energy and had worked in a senior personnel position for a large company.

Following my own advice, I called one of her previous employers and asked all of the usual questions. At the end, I asked, "Is there anything else I should know?"

He then said to me, somewhat hesitantly, "Well, she has a big company mentality." That's all he said. And because that was all he said, I ignored that hidden piece of advice and hired her for a job to be on the phone all day long working with and supporting our distributors.

After she had been on the job for a few days, she switched all of her incoming phone calls to an answering machine, which she ignored. If someone called back insistently, she had the call referred to a junior staff member to take care of it. She sat in her office and shuffled papers, avoiding contact with anyone in the field. When I called her on this, she simply insisted that she was "too busy to waste time talking to distributors who had problems or questions."

The Fatal Flaw

What her previous employer had meant by "big company mentality" was that she was very artful at delegating, at getting someone else, anyone else, to do her work for her and to never doing anything herself, personally.

When we asked her to handle any project, she would immediately farm it out to companies that charged us outrageous amounts of money for mundane tasks. On one occasion, we asked her to prepare a simple PowerPoint presentation for a meeting with clients. She gave it to a company run by a friend of hers and had a series of words on paper turned into a short PowerPoint presentation at a cost of more than $8,000. It was outrageous.

The Law of Three Revisited

Earlier, I described the Law of Three. Always interview at least three candidates. Interview the candidate you like three times, and in three different settings. Have the candidate speak to at least three other people in your company.

In checking references, you can use the Law of Three as well. Speak to at least three references provided by the job candidate. Once you have spoken to each reference, attempt to go "three deep" by asking the reference if you can speak to someone else in the company who has worked with this person. References will usually transfer you to a coworker—someone who has not been alerted to the fact that a prospective new employer will call.

Interview this coworker in detail. You will often learn things that the original reference would not tell you. Then, ask if the coworker could refer you to another person who once worked with the candidate. Very often this third person, who is completely unprepared and trusting, will give you information on the candidate that can help you make your decision, one way or the other.

Do you remember Peter Falk's TV detective character Colombo? His way of solving cases was to keep asking questions, casually and almost as if he didn't care about the answers. The more questions he asked in his casual, non-threatening way, the more vital pieces of information he acquired that enabled him to solve cases.

When you are interviewing, the more important the job is, the more of a detective you have to be. You need to be sure that the people you are considering are exactly what they appear to be. It is much, much harder to deal with people once you have hired them than it is to make the decision not to hire them in the first place.

ACTION EXERCISES

1. Resolve today that you are going to personally check at least three referrals from every job candidate from now on. This practice can save you an enormous amount of time and trouble.

2. Create a list of questions for interviewing references, just as you would for interviewing the candidate.

NINE

The Family Member Method

THE "FAMILY MEMBER METHOD" is a tool for making the final decision to hire a person for your company. It is a technique that allows you to see, think, and decide with greater clarity.

When you are thinking of hiring somebody, you ask yourself a series of questions. The first question is, "Do I like this person?" Never hire somebody that you do not *personally* like. The organizational climate in your company is made up of the mixture of personalities that you bring together. One negative person in a work environment can often poison the attitudes and performance of many other people.

The key question you should ask yourself is: "Would I be comfortable inviting this person to my home to have Sunday dinner with my family?"

Listen to the Voice in Your Head

Is this the sort of person that you would invite to your home, to sit with your family at dinner and to engage in family conversation? Would you want this person to interact with your spouse and children?

If not, why not? When you ask these questions, you will usually trigger an intuitive response. It is important to trust this "still, small voice." It will seldom lead you astray.

Sigmund Freud, then one of the most respected intellectuals in Europe, was once in a situation where he had to make an important decision. He pulled a one shilling coin out of his pocket and flicked it into the air, catching it on the back of his hand. The person he was talking to immediately asked, "Are you going to make a decision as important as this by flipping a coin?"

Freud replied, "When I flip a coin to decide yes or no, it is when the coin is in the air that I know the answer. When the coin is in the air, I know how I want it to land."

Think About Your Children

There is another good question you can ask, similar to flipping a coin into the air: "Would you put your son or daughter to work under this person or with this person?" If not, then why not?

Another question you can ask yourself is: "Would I like to spend twenty years working with this person?"

Think of having to work with and for this person for the next twenty years, seeing and conversing with him every day. Imagine being stuck in a box or a small room with this person for an extended period of time. How would you feel about that?

These questions allow you to bring the candidate into sharper focus in your own mind, almost like adjusting a camera lens to get a better picture.

If your answer to any of these questions is no, then you should assume that this is probably a wrong choice. You must always pick people that you feel comfortable with and positive about, almost to the point that you would want them to be members of your family, both in the office and at home.

When I took a graduate course in personnel selection, the professor introduced us to a series of techniques, tests, questions, and exercises for making a good hire. But at the end of the program, he told us that, in the final analysis, always trust your "gut instinct." The main purpose of all the tests and interviews is for you to acquire enough information so that your intuition will give you the right guidance to make the right decision.

ACTION EXERCISES

1. Imagine bringing a job candidate home to have dinner with your family on a Sunday evening. Imagine bringing home a member of your current staff.

2. Think about working with a staff member for the next twenty years. How do you feel about that?

TEN

The Best Predictor of Success

ONE OF MY clients was a major international accounting firm, perhaps the largest in the world, with 120,000 employees in dozens of countries. The company's managers told me of an internal study they had conducted covering thousands of employees who had worked with them over a thirty-year period, going back to their first interviews. The study examined why they decided to hire each candidate in the first place and the success of each candidate over the years.

What they discovered was quite interesting. They found that one of the top characteristics that most predicted the success of a candidate working for this major multinational firm was that the individual really wanted to work with this company, and to work nowhere else.

Self-Selection

This attitude is called "self-selection." As it happened, they only interviewed top people with excellent grades from the best universities. These candidates had the option to go to work for a variety of different companies. But the candidates who succeeded in the long term had concluded after the interviewing process that they really wanted to work for that company.

Desire is the key. The individual comes to you, after meeting with you two or three times, and says, "I really want this job! I want to work here! I don't want to work for any other company but this company. I want to make this company my career."

This is exactly what you are looking for. If a person really wants to work for your company, this is a very good predictor of long-term success in the job.

Hiring the Best

How do you encourage or elicit an attitude of self-selection? Begin at the beginning. Start by describing the job completely to the candidate, what will be expected, the goals and opportunities, and then make no offer or effort to hire him. Instead, encourage him to think it over.

Say something like, "You seem like a pretty good person. It seems like this job might be a good fit for you. Why don't you think it over for a while and call me in a couple of days and tell me what you think."

In other words, no matter how attractive the candidate, practice "reverse psychology," encouraging the other person to take some time to think about it, discuss the job with his or her spouse, and give it some consideration, with no pressure or urgency.

Some people say that if you find the right candidate, you should grab the person right away. I don't agree. A wise man I used to work for, who started from scratch and built a fortune of more than a billion dollars, once told me, "Opportunities and people for jobs are like buses. There will always be another one that comes along. You don't have to run after them and you don't have to worry. Always go slowly when you make long-term decisions."

Refuse to Be Pressured

If people try to pressure you by saying that they need a decision right away because they have another job offer, you simply say, "Okay, you should take the other job offer." If a candidate is willing to accept the most immediate offer that's available, that person will probably not work out for you in the long term.

Once the candidate has thought it over and he comes back to tell you that he really wants to work with your company, ask him, "Why do you want to work here?" The answer should be something like, "I really like this company, and I know I can do a good job here."

You then ask, "Specifically, how do you feel you could contribute?" What you are seeking is some thoughtful and intelligent ways that this candidate could make a valuable contribution.

Ask the question, "If you were to get this job, what would be the first thing you would want to do? Where would you want to start, based on everything that I've told you?"

The person who can answer these questions well is halfway home toward being a good employee. The fact that he has an intelligent answer means that he is already thinking about his contribution.

Choose Your Own Job

There is a successful company in New York that has a most remarkable hiring process. Using the Law of Three (or more) interviews, the company's managers take the candidate through a series of discussions, and when they finally decide to hire him, they let him choose his own job.

They send the candidate back out into the factory and tell him to walk around and talk to different people doing various jobs. The candidate is encouraged to keep doing this until he finds a job he likes and a team of people that he would enjoy working with. He then stops wandering around and starts working. This is the ultimate in "self-selection."

Using this system, they have an amazing record of high productivity and low turnover. This may not be appropriate for your company, but it is an approach to think about. Very often, you can hire an excellent person who turns out to be more suitable for a different job than the one you hired him for—a job where he can contribute far more value to your company. I have experienced this personally several times over the years.

ACTION EXERCISES

1. Write down a series of questions you can ask to determine if the candidate really wants the job you are offering.

2. Take a poll of some of your best employees and ask them exactly why they decided to come to work for you and your company.

ELEVEN

How to Negotiate the Salary

SALARY NEGOTIATIONS, like all negotiations, require that you get as much information as possible before you begin. There is nothing more important than accurate knowledge about the job and how much others are being paid to do it.

Your goal is to "buy" the very highest quality and quantity of labor for the very best price, the maximum that you need to pay in a competitive market.

There are many studies available on the Internet that show the salary range of a particular job, occupation, or profession. In each city, business groups and the Chamber of Commerce produce salary schedules that give the ranges that other companies are paying for a particular job in that geographical area.

Especially if you are hiring for a new or different job, be sure to find out what other companies are paying and what benefits they are offering. The power is always on the side of the person with the best information.

Pay the Price

You can be sure that when a candidate comes to interview with you for a job, he already knows how much the job is worth. Your goal is to determine how much the job should pay and to get the person to take the job at the lowest possible price, at least initially.

Past income is usually the best indicator of what you will have to pay to hire the new person for this job. If it is not on the application, ask him directly how much he earned in his previous job.

What I have found is that each person has a financial comfort level, and if you hire people at salaries below those levels, they will not be happy at their work. They will be continually thinking about money and about their bills.

Usually, people's financial comfort levels will be within a range, and your goal is to pay them toward the bottom of that range and then offer them increases based on performance.

Always specify a ninety-day trial or probationary period. Explain to candidates that at any time during the next ninety days, you can mutually decide that this job is not working out. Tell your new hires that, at the end of ninety days, you will review their salaries and benefits and decide whether they are going to stay, and if so, how much more they will be paid.

Pay Them What They Are Worth Now

Some years ago, I asked my outside accountant to help me find an inside accountant for my fast-growing business. He eventually sent me three candidates, each of whom he had screened in advance. The order of the candidates was quite clever. The first two were either partially or totally unacceptable, but the third candidate was an older woman who was absolutely excellent. Since she had already been screened, I offered her the job.

When I asked her how much she wanted, she told me that her last job paid $2,400 per month. I told her that I was only planning to pay about $1,600 a month at the beginning, but in her case, I would pay her $2,000 per month with the understanding that in ninety days we would review her performance and give her an increase at that time. She accepted this "negotiation" with some reluctance and agreed to take the job.

This was on a Friday. She came into work on the following Monday. Within one day, she had taken complete control of our out-of-control finances and accounting. On Tuesday morning, I walked in and increased her salary to $2,400 per month. For the rest of the time she worked for me, I would walk in twice a year and give her a preemptive increase to a higher salary. She deserved it.

My point is that if you have hired truly excellent people, forget about ninety-day job reviews and increase their pay immediately. The most expensive person in the world of work is a highly talented person who you allow to be hired away by someone else for a few dollars more. Remember that the very best people are usually working somewhere else. They already have jobs. They already have paychecks and job security. To get the very best people for your business, you're usually going to have to hire them away.

Good People Are "Free"

Don't be reluctant to pay well for talented people. Excellent, highly productive people will contribute far more value to your company than you can pay them in salary and benefits.

In Economics 101, you learn about the Law of Marginal Utility. This law says that a company adds new people as long as each new person more than pays for himself, either in increased profitability or decreased costs, or both. Good people are therefore "free" (though poor performers can be very expensive).

In employing people, you generally tend to get exactly what you paid for. As my friend Ken Blanchard once said, "If you pay peanuts, you get monkeys."

ACTION EXERCISES

1. Think of every new hire as an investment from which you are required to earn a profit, an excess of income over total expense.

2. Show all new hires what they will have to do, either in terms of increasing revenues, bringing about cost savings, or making contributions that are greater than their costs.

TWELVE

Start Them Off Right

WE DISCUSSED earlier that one of the qualities that is more predictive of long-term success in a job than any others is "self-selection"—when the candidate really wants to work for this one company, more than any other company that he might have chosen or that might have chosen him.

The same research uncovered a second quality that predicts success: the way the individual starts the job, from the very first day. As the saying goes, "Well begun is half done."

People today are too valuable for the "sink-or-swim method." New employees require a "hands-on approach" in their new jobs. Start your people off right.

When a person begins a new job they have what is called "low task-relevant maturity." This means that they don't yet know how to do the job properly. They have limited or no knowledge or experience of this job. They may have an excellent education and may have done many other jobs in the past, but at this job, they are brand new, almost like infants.

High Willingness, Low Confidence

On the first day, your new employees' willingness is high but their self-confidence is low. It is at this special moment in their career that they need a lot of hands-on attention from you or from someone else. This is the key to building high-performing employees.

Most companies and managers have onboarding plans for new hires, especially expensive and important new employees. But even if you are starting an administrative assistant or receptionist, it is absolutely essential that you have a plan, a checklist, of exactly your process for quickly getting this person up to speed.

You should organize your time so that you or someone else can work closely with new employees for the first few days or weeks, familiarizing them with the past, present, and future of the company and with their particular jobs. Many companies have a complete one- or two-week process of familiarization that they go through with each new employee or groups of new employees. This is especially important if your company is growing fast and you are bringing new people on board at a rapid rate.

Assign Them to Top People

If you do not have the time to work closely with new employees, assign them to one of your best people. Some companies make the mistake of assigning a new employee to an average or underperforming employee, thinking that this is a good use of the mediocre employee's time. However, it is during the first few days and weeks of the job when the new employee develops an understanding of how the company works, the required standards of performance, and the competence of the other people.

When you assign an average or underperforming employee to show the new person the ropes, the new employee quickly gets the impression that average performance is all that is expected in the company. If you assign a new employee to a person who does not work very hard or well, or who is negative and complaining, the new employee will adopt these behaviors and this mind-set from the very beginning. This is not what you had in mind.

Use a Buddy System

When you set up a buddy system for the new employee, you should sit down with the employee who is going to orient the new person and work out a strategy and plan of action, even just a checklist, for exactly what you want the current employee to do in the first few days and weeks with the new employee. Do not leave this to chance.

Good people are too valuable, expensive, and important for you to go through all the trouble of hiring them and then let them start slowly with average performers as their models for their own performance in the future.

What companies have found is that even ten years after their hiring, if employees are started off right, with intense training with top people in their first few weeks and months, they are far, far ahead of other people who started at the same time but who did not get the initial high-quality, hands-on training and treatment.

The Lowest-Performing Companies

As a sales manager and trainer over the years, I have been amazed to learn that fully 70 percent of companies do no sales training at all. They do what is called "product training," and they think that this is the same as teaching people how to approach and interact with a prospective customer.

When I worked with IBM as an outside speaker and trainer, I was delighted to find that after the company had gone through the laborious process of selecting a new salesperson, it would train that salesperson for as long as eighteen months before the salesperson was allowed to go out into the field and contact customers on his own.

The best companies start their new people with intense training, like the Marine Corps, to make sure that their new people become excellent and important contributors to the company for the long term.

Take Your Time

Future performance is significantly improved when an employee is started right, from the first day.

The best companies are those that take the onboarding process very seriously. They plan it carefully in advance. They commit their very best people to it. They stay on top of the process and maintain an open-door policy. They invite the new employees to go to their managers at any time with any questions or concerns, especially before they lose their confidence and enthusiasm.

ACTION EXERCISES

1. Take the time to assign or partner a new person in a new job with someone who can show the new hire what to do.

2. Develop a written plan for exactly what you will do to start a new employee off right.

THIRTEEN

Start Them Strong

NEW EMPLOYEES are usually eager, willing, and ready to get into their new jobs and get going. You should therefore bury them in work from the first morning. Give new employees lots to do. Work overload makes the job challenging and exciting.

Don't give your new hires ninety days to settle in and feel their way around the company. Pile the work on right from the beginning and give them plenty of feedback and help. Give them lots of opportunity for discussion and asking questions.

No Time to Relax

Some years ago, I had applied to work for the senior executive of a large company. We had several previous meetings, but no final decision had been made on his part. From these conversations, he knew that I was taking graduate courses at the university to complete my MBA. He also knew that my final exam ended at 2:00 p.m. on a Thursday.

After the exam, exhausted, I went home to my apartment, full of happiness and relief that the two solid years of study was at an end. At three o'clock the phone rang. When I answered it, it was the senior executive calling to say that he had decided to offer me the position. I was both grateful and delighted. I knew this was a great opportunity for me to use all of my recent education, plus all my previous experience.

When Can You Start?

Since it was Thursday, my thought was that he would want me to start on Monday, giving me three days to decompress from the two years of study. I asked him, "When would you like me to start?"

He replied, "How about right now? How long will it take you to get in to the office?"

I assured him that I would be there within the hour. I quickly changed into a suit, which was the standard dress for people in that company, and drove hurriedly over to the office to meet with my new boss.

He pulled out a sheet of paper and said, "I've made a list of projects that I want you to start on right away. Here it is."

From that moment on and for the next two years, I worked ten- to fourteen-hour days, traveling constantly, eventually handling three divisions of the company, and working seven days a week. The more work I did, the more work he gave me to do. There was no respite or opportunity to slow down.

The Best Learning Experience

The best news was that I learned more in those two unbroken years of work than I might have learned in ten or twenty years working for a company at a slower pace. It was easily the best work experience of my life. It benefited me tremendously, and it benefited the company equally as much. It was a win-win for everyone.

To this day, I look back with gratitude for the fact that my new boss got me up and working quickly and never let off the pressure.

On the first day on the job, the new employee is most open to new possibilities and new challenges. Take advantage of this positive attitude. On the other hand, there is nothing more disheartening than starting a new job full of hope and anticipation and then being forced to sit around for several days or weeks while the company allows you to get oriented and become comfortable.

Meet the Coworkers

When the new person starts, introduce her to everyone with whom she will work. Explain how the company operates. Welcome the new employee as a new member of your corporate family, and then bury them in work.

Employees may complain about how much work they have to do, and they may be tired out when they are leaving at six or seven at night, but in their hearts, they love every minute of it.

There is a lot of talk and complaining about companies making their employees work and overwork today. However, when employees are surveyed, they rank "being active, involved, and busy all day long" as one of the best qualities of an excellent job. The worst thing they can say is that they are sitting around bored, with not enough to do. People like to be busy.

ACTION EXERCISES

1. Make a list of several jobs that you need done and assign them to a new person. It is never too late.

2. Arrange to get whatever additional training and guidance employees need to do new jobs. The sooner you train them, the sooner your time will be free for more valuable tasks.

FOURTEEN

Use the Correct Leadership Style

THERE IS A rule that you can never expect people to do a good job at a task if they have not been trained thoroughly on how to do the task in an excellent fashion.

Paul Hersey, in his book *The Situational Leader,* revolutionized management and the understanding of how to work with different employees with his four quadrant method.

He taught that each employee has a certain level of skill and ability in a particular job, which dictates the leadership style that is most effective in eliciting the very best results from that person.

The Telling Style

If the new person has limited knowledge or skill, or none at all, in a new job, this person requires a directing style of management. The role of the manager is to tell the person exactly what to do, to teach him how to do the new job, and to explain it to him in detail. This is leadership style number one, "Telling." Hands-on management is essential.

The Selling Style

The second leadership style in this model is "Selling." The leader is still providing the direction, but she is now using two-way communication and both encouraging and motivating the individual to do the job.

The Participating Style

The third leadership style is called "Participating," and it's when the leader invites questions and feedback about the job and the best way to get it done. Commitment to task accomplishment is in direct proportion to the amount of time the employee has to discuss the work in advance.

The Delegating Style

The fourth and highest level of management, "Delegating," is when the leader is still involved in decisions, but the process and responsibility has been passed to the now experienced individual or group. The leader stays involved to monitor progress, but assigns the job and allows other people to do it.

The correct leadership style depends on the relative skill and experience of the employee. A key insight of situational leadership is that often, when a new person with previous experience comes into the company, the manager makes the mistake that the previous level of experience is completely transferable to the new job. Instead of using a *directing* style of leadership, the manager, as busy as he is, uses a *delegating* style of leadership—in effect leaving the new employee with no direction.

Our New Receptionist

Some years ago, we went through our hiring process and chose a new receptionist for our fast-growing business. The new receptionist was to replace our old receptionist, who was moving on to a better position more consistent with her education.

We practiced the Law of Three and had multiple people interview this new woman. We were both impressed with her and convinced that she would do an excellent job. But after one day on the job, the previous receptionist, who had stayed on to train the new receptionist, came to us and told us that we had made a terrible mistake. The new person was completely incompetent. She could not do the job and should be replaced at once.

I was quite surprised. Then I asked her a key question, "Have you thoroughly trained her in every part of the new job, including how to use our telephone system, computer, and related software?"

She said, surprised, "No, I haven't. I assumed that if she was being hired for the job, she would already know how to do it."

I then asked her to go back to the new employee and patiently teach her everything she needed to know to operate our systems, which were quite new. The old receptionist reluctantly agreed to do so.

An Amazing Transformation

With one week of training, the new receptionist turned out to be absolutely excellent. She was easily the best and most competent person at that job that any of us had ever seen. But she wasn't on the first day because she had not been trained in how to do the job properly. She stayed with us for several years, until she married and moved away.

What she needed was a "directing," hands-on style of management until she learned the new job and acquired enough competence to be able to function on her own.

Remember, it costs a lot of time and money to go through the process of selecting employees and then lose them because you had not thought through the process of managing them correctly at each stage of their becoming familiar with the job.

ACTION EXERCISES

1. Think about your employees and note where you might be experiencing problems and frustrations. Could it be that you are using the wrong leadership style based on the person's level of competence and familiarity with the job?

2. Experiment with the leadership styles of "telling, selling, participating, and delegating" with different people. Remember, "Different strokes for different folks."

FIFTEEN

Improve Performance Continually

IT IS ESTIMATED that, especially in a growing company, one-third of new hires will do an excellent job. One-third will be average performers, and one-third will turn out to be the wrong people for the job, either in the short term or later on, as the company and the job changes.

For this reason, you are going to have performance problems as regularly as breathing in and breathing out. One of your chief responsibilities as a manager is to address performance problems and to ensure that each person on the payroll is making a maximum contribution to the company. Firing an employee is a last resort. When performance problems arise, if you demonstrate your true leadership qualities and your real ability to manage people effectively, you will help people improve their performance and avoid the pain of being fired.

The Best Jobs

In one study, when employees were asked to cite the best job they ever had, they would each recall a particular company and boss. The next question was, "Why was this the best job that you ever had?"

The two most common answers to this question were, "I always felt that the boss cared about me as a person," and "I always knew what was expected of me."

Perhaps the best way to ensure the best performance is to offer clear, confident, positive expectations. Employees should know exactly what you want them to do, and to what standard, by what date, and how excellent performance is to be measured.

If people do not have clear key result areas, and do not know what to do and to what standard, their performance will often start to drift.

When people have a clear job and can measure their progress toward doing that job in an excellent fashion, they experience a continual source of motivation that drives them forward.

The second key to performance improvement is regular feedback. Ken Blanchard says, "Feedback is the breakfast of champions!"

People start to lose their motivation and commitment when they don't get regular feedback or opportunites to talk to their bosses on a regular basis.

A Great Place to Work

Each year, the researchers at the Great Place to Work Institute compile a report in which they ask employees how they feel about their jobs.

One of the most common responses, year after year, for top companies is that people feel free to speak up to their bosses—that is, to express their thoughts, feelings, and opinions and have their bosses listen to them and even take action on their suggestions. Above all, employees felt that they could speak up or disagree without any fear of criticism or of losing their jobs.

One of your main jobs is to give regular feedback to employees and tell them how well they are doing. Give them ideas and suggestions to do their jobs better.

Inspect Things Regularly

The third key to performance improvement is to "inspect what you expect." An important key to managerial success is to keep on top of things by regularly checking to see how the work is going. Just like a doctor making the rounds each morning, you must keep your hands on the pulse of your business.

Practice "management by wandering around." Wander around and talk to each person each day, or more than once each day, to see how your employees are doing. Do they have any problems or questions? Is there anything that you can do to help them do their jobs better? Offer to give help, and to give feedback, counsel, and advice. Offer to get them additional resources if they need them to do their jobs.

When you assign clear work tasks, provide feedback, and then regularly check with people to see how they are doing, you are telling them that their work is important. If their work is important, then by extension, they are important people as well.

Never Assume

The fourth key to performance improvement is to never assume anything. Never assume that people understand or know what's going on. Never assume that they completely understand what they are supposed to do. Continually talk about the work with your employees and invite them to ask questions and give you feedback, too. You will often be surprised at the difference between their perception of the work you want them to do and your perception.

Express Yourself Clearly

On two occasions, I was very frustrated with certain people who were working for me. They were not doing the jobs that I wanted them to do, and they were not doing them well. I became angrier and angrier, taking my problems home and grousing about them over dinner. One evening, my wife asked, "Have you told these people exactly what you are thinking and feeling about their work?"

I said, "Of course not! They are mature people. I assume that they know what they are supposed to be doing and why I am unhappy."

She said, "Why don't you sit them down and tell them exactly what you have been telling me? You may be surprised."

My wife was right. I took the employees at different times into my office and laid out clearly why I was frustrated by each of their performances. In both cases, they were shocked and surprised. They had no idea that they were not doing their jobs the way they were expected to do them. They had no idea that I or anyone else was dissatisfied or unhappy.

In both cases, they immediately promised that they would make whatever changes were necessary to do their jobs in an excellent fashion. And they both did. I learned a valuable lesson from that, too. Never assume that the other person knows why you are unhappy if you have not sat down with the person and clearly spelled it out.

You can improve most performance problems by giving clear direction and regular feedback, by inspecting what you expect, and by not assuming anything.

ACTION EXERCISES

1. Practice management by wandering around. Get up from behind your desk and walk around, asking questions, listening, and checking on how things are going.

2. Hold weekly meetings, even daily huddles, to ensure that everyone knows what everyone else is doing. This practice dramatically increases morale and team spirits.

SIXTEEN

Address Performance Problems

YOU HAVE NOW selected the right people, started them off right, given them lots of work to do, and have provided them with all the training and resources that they need to do an excellent job. Regardless, you are going to have performance problems. It is the nature of work, and an essential part of being a manager.

Somehow, the job is not getting done, the employee is not getting along with others, or there are problems with the quality of the work that are having negative downstream effects. The individual might not be coming to work on time or is causing disharmony and unhappiness in the office as the result of criticizing, complaining, or displaying other forms of negativity.

Discuss Them Immediately

The starting point of dealing with performance problems is to address them immediately. Take the person into your office, close the door, and discuss your concerns away from others, without interruptions. Tell the employee that you are not happy with his performance or behavior in a particular area and then ask him, "What seems to be the problem?"

Be specific and give concrete examples. Say something like, "You have been late three times this week—fifteen, twenty-five, and forty-five minutes late. I'd like to know what the problem is."

Before you confront an employee, be sure that you have correct information. If someone tells you, "So and so did this and that," find out for sure beforehand. Get the facts. Then, repeat back what you have heard, without emotion or judgment, and invite the employee to respond. Hear him or her out. Listen carefully, without commenting or interrupting, to the employee's side of the problem or situation.

Agree on a Solution

After you have had this discussion and it is clear to both of you that a performance problem exists, focus on the solution, on what can be done to ensure that this problem does not arise again. Agree on how performance is to be improved and by how much. Agree on what is to be done, and when. You can say, "Okay, you have been late several times this week. What are you going to do about this?" Or, "You are having problems with the people down in shipping. What can we do to resolve this situation?"

Ask the employee to agree to be on time from now on. Ask the employee to deal straightforwardly with the other people with whom he or she is having problems. Get agreement that the employee will take specific actions to solve these problems immediately.

Monitor and Follow Up

After this discussion, you monitor and follow up. You give feedback and support or additional help if necessary. You make sure that the employee does what he agreed to do in your meeting. Check and make sure. Never assume.

Keep accurate notes and records on this type of discussion. Make notes about what was discussed and agreed to. You may even share these notes with the employee. Then put your notes into the individual's file. This is an important step because it protects you, should it become necessary to let this person go later.

Four Major Issues

There are four issues that might arise with an employee that can lead to performance problems. Once you recognize them, you can quickly resolve them, if these are the reasons that the employee is not performing in the first place.

1. Role Confusion. The employee does not know what she is expected to do; this is often the major issue behind poor performance.

2. Role Contradiction. In this situation, if the employee does one job, he will not be able to do another job. If he is expected to complete copious paperwork, he cannot be calling on customers and making sales.

3. Role Overlap. The employee is expected to do all or part of a job that somebody else is expected to do all or part of as well. In this case, either both employees try to do the job and conflict, or neither employee does it, assuming that the other one will do it. The rule is that every job must be assigned clearly and specifically to a single person. Sometimes this is as easy to do as writing out specifically what each person is expected to contribute. Clarity is your best friend.

4. Role Underlap. There is a specific job, parts of which are assigned to two or more people, but specific parts of which are not assigned to anyone. The manager can quite quickly resolve this problem by assigning the parts of the work that are not getting done to a specific person.

Whatever the situation, begin by assuming that you are responsible for the problem, and instead of blaming or criticizing the employee, look into yourself, your management style, the employee's job description, and other things to see if there is something that you are doing (or not doing) that's causing the problem.

Remember, it is always easier to save a problem employee who is having difficulties than it is to lose them and to have to start over again with someone else.

ACTION EXERCISES

1. Examine a situation where you are having performance problems with an employee and look for reasons that the company could be causing this problem.

2. Whenever you have a performance problem of any kind, address it immediately. Very often, you can catch it early before it becomes a major misunderstanding.

SEVENTEEN

The Two Main Reasons for Employee Failure

THERE ARE many reasons why employees don't work out over time, but there are two basic reasons for which there is no cure.

Reason number one is that the person is not motivated, for whatever reason. You may hire an absolutely excellent person, but over time, or as the result of some life change, the individual loses interest in the job. These employees are now just going through the motions and collecting their paychecks, but they don't really care.

According to the research, fully 64 percent of employees are "disengaged." They have low levels of commitment or loyalty to their companies. They are constantly on the lookout for other jobs.

Four Quadrants

Jack Welch, when he was president of General Electric, wrote an article that is now taught in business schools all over the country. In it, he described his philosophy regarding the kind of people who worked at GE and what to do with them at different stages of their careers.

He divided people into four categories, using the descriptors of Competent, Not Competent, Buy In, and Don't Buy In.

QUADRANT 1

These are the people who are both competent and motivated. They "buy in" to the values and beliefs of General Electric. They are real contributors and excellent players in the business. The company is built around them.

QUADRANT 2

These are the people who are competent, but they don't buy in to the values of General Electric. They do a good job, but they feel that the company values are something separate and apart from their own ideas and behaviors.

QUADRANT 3

These are people who are not competent but who buy into General Electric values. They are positive, motivated, and require more training and experience. The company worked hard to move them into Quadrant 1.

QUADRANT 4

The fourth group of people that Jack Welch identified are those who are neither competent at their work, nor believe in General Electric values. These people are let go by the company as quickly as possible.

The Major Conclusion

What made this article so impactful was his final conclusion. Welch said that "the people who are competent but don't buy in to the company's values were the main source of problems, misunderstandings, politics, and negativity in the company."

If people are not prepared to put their whole hearts into doing the very best jobs they possibly can, the best thing for you to do is to encourage them to go somewhere else where they can be more committed.

It is not uncommon to hire a person who does an excellent job for an extended period of time and then "goes bad" on you. Sometimes when people get married or romantically involved, this happens. They become so distracted that they no longer care about the job. People may become demotivated because of drugs or alcohol or other changes in their lives. Whatever the reason, it is time for them to move on.

Competent and Motivated

When I set up a company for a previous employer, I recruited widely and found some great people. A woman I hired to work as my general manager and secretary was excellent. She had a great attitude. She was a hard worker. She was creative and innovative. She made herself indispensable for almost two years.

Then, something went wrong in her romantic life and she "lost it." She became negative, uncooperative, unproductive, and undependable. No matter how many times I tried to talk to her and bring her back to her previous status, nothing improved. With regret, I finally had to let her go and find someone else. I learned later that this situation, an employee going from good to bad, is not an unusual occurrence.

Lack of Ability

The second main reason that people do not work out is that they are incompetent. They just can't do the job. If you have hired a person who is not competent at the job, no matter how hard he tries, you need to ask yourself who's really incompetent.

Peter Drucker said that "a manager who hires an incompetent person, and who keeps that person in place, is himself incompetent and unfit for leadership."

Who is incompetent? Is it the person without the skills, talents, or abilities and who cannot do the job, or the person who hired the incompetent person?

Unfortunately, it is the person who makes the hiring decision who is the incompetent person.

Face the Truth

The longer you keep an incompetent person in a position where it is obvious to all that he cannot do the job, the more you demoralize the people around you.

In addition, you look increasingly incompetent to your superiors and to your peers. They see you as being incapable of doing your job.

If the job has changed and the person in the job is unable to change or refuses to learn and grow to get the job done, it is your responsibility to move quickly to replace the employee.

The rule is that "everybody knows everything." Everyone knows who is competent and who is not competent. When you keep an incompetent person in place, you are in effect rewarding incompetence. By extension, you are punishing the competent people who are working hard to do their jobs by paying incompetent people on either side of them.

Lack of Motivation or Lack of Competence?

How can you tell which it is, whether a person lacks motivation or competence? There is a simple test: Ask the question, "If his life depended on it, could he do this job well?"

If the employee could not do the job well, even if his life depended on it, then it means that he is incompetent. If the employee could do the job well, if his life depended on it, then it simply means that he is not motivated. You must decide for yourself.

One poor player on a team can demoralize the entire team. The members of your team look to you to protect them, to make sure that they have other competent people to work with. This is one of your main responsibilities as a manager.

ACTION EXERCISES

1. Look at the members of your staff. Is there anyone who is doing poorly? Is it because she is incompetent or unmotivated?

2. Does everyone on your team "buy in" to your company, and are they all completely committed to your success? If not, what are you going to do about it?

EIGHTEEN

Zero-Based Thinking

THIS IS A mental tool that you can use in every part of your business, and especially with your employees.

Continually ask yourself, "Is there anything that I am doing that, knowing what I now know, I would not start up again today if I had to do it over?"

In times of turbulence and rapid change, as we are experiencing today, you will be continually dealing with past decisions and commitments that, knowing what you now know, you would not make again today.

It Seemed Like a Good Idea

When you originally made the decision, it may have been an excellent decision, based on the knowledge you had at that time. But the situation has changed. You have new knowledge and experience. The external world—your customers and competition—have changed as well. What was a good decision at one time is no longer such a great decision today. If this is the case, your job is to reverse the decision as fast as you can.

With regard to employees, you can use this mental construct continually throughout your career. Simply ask, "Is there anyone working for me who, knowing what I now know, I would not hire back or assign to that job?"

If the answer is "yes," then your next question is, "How do I get rid of this person, and how fast?"

If you have hired a person who has not worked out, move quickly to replace that person with someone who can do the job.

Evaluate Each Employee

Look at each person who reports to you and ask that question. "Knowing what I now know, would I hire this person back again?"

In my own companies and executive jobs, I have asked this question over and over. If ever someone does not pass this simple test, I move immediately to get that person out of the company. The person who you would not hire back again today is a major source of your problems and difficulties as a manager.

Remember, the manager who keeps the incompetent person in place is the one who is truly incompetent.

There is a rule: "The best time to fire a person is the first time it crosses your mind."

Be Kind and Compassionate

Many managers persuade themselves that by not firing a person, they are being compassionate and kind. They are somehow doing people favors by keeping them in jobs to which they are clearly unsuited.

They see themselves as humanitarians, kind and understanding, not willing to do something that might hurt the incompetent person. But this is really not the case. The primary reason that managers do not fire someone is cowardice. The manager who refrains from firing a person who is obviously unsuited for the job is not demonstrating character or kindness, but rather a form of spinelessness, which is unfortunately too common in business today.

In addition, keeping people in jobs that are wrong for them is a form of cruelty. The most precious resource that a person has is his time. If it is clear that someone has no real future at a particular job, the kindest, most compassionate, and generous thing you can do is to set that person free to can go and find a job that is more suitable.

At the same time, the coldest, most heartless, devastating, and unkind thing you can do is to keep people working at jobs where they have no futures. Sooner or later, the end will come. And all those extra months and even years that the individual has worked at the job will be completely wasted time and wasted life—both irretrievable.

Do the Right Thing

It is important that managers not fool themselves into thinking that they have some high level of character or virtue when they avoid firing an obviously incompetent person. It is merely weakness and cowardice that holds them back from "doing the right thing."

ACTION EXERCISES

1. Review all the people who work for you and determine if there is anyone you would not hire back again today, if they walked in and applied for their current jobs.

2. If there is anyone working for you who does not pass this simple test, resolve to help the person move on to a more appropriate job as soon as possible.

NINETEEN

When Firing Becomes Inevitable

WHEN FIRING is inevitable, be prepared to protect yourself and your company. I have studied many books on this subject and have developed my own method for firing that is both simple and effective. Over the years, I've shared my method with thousands of managers who have gone back to their offices that day and fired problem employees. None of them have ever been sued.

The starting point in professional firing is for you to prepare thoroughly. When it comes to firing, especially with the number of lawyers who work on straight commission today, trolling for clients and looking for companies from which they can extort settlements, you must be very careful.

At Will Employment

In the United States, most employment is "at will." This means that almost anyone can be fired at almost any time, with or without a reason. Nonetheless, the average wrongful termination suit costs a company between $75,000 and $100,000. This is because the manager acts precipitously and fires someone without preparing thoroughly in advance.

No matter how you feel, you don't just walk in and say, "You're fired." Instead, take your time. Make a case. Assemble the necessary documentation with regard to performance records, disciplinary discussions, absenteeism, and other problems that have occurred with this person.

The most powerful tool you can have when letting someone go is a paper trail of documented discussions about performance problems that you have had with this person.

Keep a Paper Trail

The general rule for firing is: "One, two, three, and you're out." What this means is that if you have documented performance reviews with the failing employee at least three times, and you make notes at each of these meetings and put them in the employee's file, it is almost impossible for the employee to then sue you and claim that they were given no warning or opportunity to improve their performance.

What is even better is that when you have three performance reviews, each signed by yourself and the employee, there is virtually no lawyer who will take the case on a contingency basis. Lawyers only accept commission-only cases when they feel that there is a chance to extort money from the company. When you practice "three times and you're out," the lawyers won't go near it unless the employee pays them a large and nonrefundable retainer.

Think About Litigation

When you let a person go, you have to, as they say, "Do it for the judge." Do it in such a way that if it came to trial or went to court, the case you make would convince a judge. If you do this, it will never get to court.

When you have to let someone go, it is important that you do it with as little emotion as possible. Never fire when you are angry. Take some time to calm down. Take some time to relax. You need to be in complete control of your emotions during the firing discussion.

There is a saying: "The most stressful part of a manager's life is being fired. The second most stressful part of a manager's life is firing someone else. And if you don't get some experience with the second, unfortunately, you're going to get some experience with the first."

Review It in Your Mind

Review the firing scenario by going over it in your mind. Think on paper. Write it down. Plan it thoroughly, step by step and even word by word. Be sure to discuss it with someone else. Ask for insights and ideas from someone whose opinion you respect. Sometimes another person acting as a sounding board can give you helpful insights on what you're contemplating and give you some good advice. You may be approaching the firing in the wrong way, or your evidence may be too weak. Don't rely solely on your own judgment.

Prepare a severance package in advance. Be clear about what you are going to offer the person as severance before you go into the firing interview. Don't put yourself in the position of having to negotiate the severance package at the same time you are firing the person. This puts you at a tremendous disadvantage.

Finally, summon your courage and resolve to do what must be done. Make the decision to terminate the employee and then remain resolute. Don't let anything or anyone change your mind.

William James once wrote, "The starting point in dealing with any difficulty is to be willing to have it so."

Once you have determined that this is the decision that has to be made, an enormous amount of your stress and tension will evaporate. You are now ready to take the final step.

ACTION EXERCISES

1. If there is someone working for you who you know is not going to work out, begin preparing for the firing process by meeting with the individual and explaining that you are not satisfied with the individual's performance, and exactly why not.

2. Give the unsatisfactory employee clear instructions regarding what he or she must do to perform the job satisfactorily, and by when, and then write it down right then and there. Ask the employee to sign the document.

TWENTY

The Firing Interview

FIRING IS always stressful, but it is essential to the growth of an excellent organization. It is what pruning is to a gardener and to a plant of any kind. It is something that has to be done as an organization grows and changes.

The best time for the firing interview is on Monday, Tuesday, or Wednesday, first thing in the morning or last thing at the end of the day. Whenever possible, don't fire someone on a Thursday and especially not on a Friday. This gives the fired person the entire weekend to become angrier and angrier. This anger can often lead to irrational behavior, unnecessary lawsuits, and even worse behaviors. When you fire earlier in the week, the person can walk out and start looking for a new job immediately.

Always choose a location for firing other than in your own office. Afterward, you want to be able to get up and leave. Go to the employee's office or to a meeting room. If you don't have a meeting room, then take the employee out for coffee to deliver the news.

Finally, don't beat around the bush. Be direct. Come straight to the point.

Repeat These Words

Here is the technique that I use: Once you have decided to let someone go, you sit down with the person and say these words: "Joe (or Susan), I have given your job situation a lot of thought. And I have decided that this is not the right job for you, and that you are not the right person for this job. And I think you would be happier doing something else."

Once you have decided to let the person go, your job is to be respectful and to protect the other person's self-esteem. This is a sensitive moment. When people are fired from jobs, even jobs that they hate, their self-esteem plunges. It goes through the floor.

Refuse to Discuss the Past

Avoid blaming or rehashing past work experience. Refuse to recite a list of all the things that the person has done or not done. It is too late for that. It is over. The person's job is finished. Avoid any temptation to make the fired employee feel guilty for anything done or not done in the past.

Instead, just keep repeating the magic words, over and over. "I don't think that this is the right job for you, and you are not the right person for this job, and I think you would be happier doing something else."

Job Loss Is Usually No Surprise

Many employees, as many as 70 percent, are aware that they are about to be fired. It is clear to them that the job is not working out. They are not happy. You are not happy, and their coworkers are not happy. There is a sense of inevitability about the situation.

However, in our litigious society, people who think that they may soon be fired can very quickly "lawyer up." They can find a lawyer directly, or through a friend, and get counsel on exactly how to handle the potential firing interview. The lawyer will tell them exactly how to provoke you into saying things and into rehashing past events, opening up opportunities for you to be sued. Don't fall into this trap.

Once employees are assured that you are not going to recite a list of their mistakes and deficiencies, lower their self-esteem, blame them, or leave them feeling guilty and incompetent, they will finally settle down and stop arguing. You can then move on to the next part of the firing interview.

The Severance Package

The severance package should be designed to reduce the immediate trauma of losing a job. The basic reason for the package is to act as a bridge between their current job and their next job.

Fully 70 percent of adults have no savings in the bank.

They live from paycheck to paycheck. The greatest fear people have when they're fired is that they are going to run out of money and won't be able to pay their bills.

The best thing that you can do in the firing interview is to make it crystal clear that they will be okay and they won't run out of money.

The Severance Amount

The basic rule is that if a person has only been working with you for a short period of time, one to two weeks' severance pay is sufficient. If a person has been working for more than two years, add one week per year of employment. This varies a bit across different industries and businesses, but one week per year is the standard.

The best way to structure the severance package is the same way as payroll. If you are giving twelve weeks of severance, give it to them one or two weeks at a time, the same way you would pay them if they were still working for you. This delayed payment option is a bulwark against the individual attempting to sue you or to badmouth you in the marketplace.

You can also offer to maintain the ex-employee's health insurance. This gives people a cushion and some peace of mind. You can also offer a letter of reference, which talks about the good things the person did on the job and leaves out everything else. Very often, the employee will leave peacefully if there is severance pay, continued health benefits, and a letter of reference as part of the package.

Another thing you can do in an amicable settlement is to

provide private outplacement counseling, especially for executives and managers with long tenure. This is quite standard in large companies. You may even have an out-placement counselor available to help the individual to secure a new job.

Act Immediately

If the parting is acrimonious or the person gets angry and threatens to sue or get back at you, have the person escorted out of your place of business immediately. Have someone standing by to take this person to their desk, clear it out, leave the keys and credit cards, and exit the building. If it turns out this way, you must treat the person the same way you would pluck a wasp off your skin. The longer the person stays, the more dangerous the situation can be.

When I fire someone, I always have another person in attendance at the firing interview, usually the same gender as the person being fired. Always have a witness who sits there and listens to every word so that there are no misunderstandings later.

Create a Cover Story

Assuming that it is a friendly parting, agree on what is called "the cover story." The cover story is how you protect the self-esteem and reputation of the person you are firing. The cover story is what you will tell other people if they ask you. You will say, "Joe (or Susan) left for this reason."

You can ask them if they would like to resign for personal reasons. Suggest that they write a letter of resignation so that they can tell people that they resigned or quit on their own volition, because they were no longer happy with the opportunities at your company, or that they wanted to do something else with their lives. It doesn't really matter. It is a face-saving device. Once you agree on a cover story, you must never tell anyone else anything except what the two of you have agreed to say.

Your goal in the severance conversation is to make the firing as friendly and as low key as possible. Make it easy and smooth. Be as gentle and as fair as possible, and when the firing is over, get up and leave.

ACTION EXERCISES

1. Review this chapter carefully, make a checklist, and practice these ideas the next time you have to fire someone. The better you become at firing, the better a manager you will be.

2. Overcome your natural fear or hesitation in firing by summoning up your courage and doing what needs to be done. After that, it becomes easier and easier.

TWENTY-ONE

The Zen of Firing

ALMOST EVERYONE gets fired at one time or another during the course of a career. And almost everyone has to fire someone in the course of a career. The Zen of firing refers to the expression, "What goes around comes around." If you have to fire a person, remember that there is a law of sowing and reaping in the universe. This is the iron law of human destiny, which is never broken.

When you fire a person, be fair. Be kind. Be generous and empathetic. Err on the side of gentleness and compassion. When you have to fire a person, you are in a position of tremendous power. Recognize this, and don't abuse it.

Even if the fired person is upset, angry, and lashing out, and even if he has been a problem for you for a long time and you are thoroughly fed up with him, you must still be gentle. Remember, as they say, "Life is very long."

The Golden Rule

Practice the Golden Rule. "Do unto others as you would have others do unto you." Fire other people the way that you would like to be fired, when and if it ever becomes your turn.

Once you go through the stress of the firing interview, the fired person is going to be upset. However, in most cases he is probably going to get a new job that he likes better and you will turn out to be right. He will get a job where he is happier.

When people have reached a point where they have to be fired, they've also reached the point where they are not happy with their work anyway. In many cases, if you fire properly, the person will come back and thank you later.

Remain on a Friendly Basis

I still see many people socially that I have had to fire. They still have me at their homes for holidays and dinners, and I still have them in my home.

In almost every case, they are doing something they enjoy far more, they are earning more money, and they have often told me that being let go by me was the best thing that ever happened to them.

When you fire somebody, keep in mind the fact that because of the way the world works, you may one day find yourself applying to that person for a job. You may find yourself working for the person that you fired years before. You may find yourself needing that person's referral or testimonial or influence at some time later in your career.

These situations are more common than you realize. When you have to let people go, always do it gently and respectfully, so they remain your friends and supporters.

Firing is stressful, but it can be done with grace and dignity. The final result will be that you, the individual, and the company will be better off.

Treat people you're firing as though they may be influential to your career in the future. Be professional, firm, kind, positive, and gentle. Remember the Zen of firing. Practice the Golden Rule. If you have to do it, do it right.

"Inspiring, entertaining, informative, motivational . . ."

Brian Tracy is one of the world's top speakers. He addresses more than 250,000 people annually—in over 100 appearances—and has consulted and trained at more than 1,000 corporations. In his career he has reached over five million people in 58 countries. He has lived and practiced every principle in his writing and speeches:

21st-Century Thinking: How to out-maneuver the competition and get superior results in an ever-turbulent business climate.

Leadership in the New Millennium: Learn the most powerful leadership principles—ever—to get maximum results, faster.

Advanced Selling Strategies: How to use modern sales' most advanced strategies and tactics to outperform your competitors.

The Psychology of Success: Think and act like the top performers. Learn practical proven techniques for excellence.

To book Brian to speak at your next meeting or conference, visit Brian Tracy International at www.briantracy.com, or call (858)436-7316 for a free promotional package. Brian will carefully customize his talk to your specific needs.

ABOUT THE AUTHOR

Brian Tracy is a professional speaker, trainer, seminar leader, and consultant, and chairman of Brian Tracy International, a training and consulting company based in Solana Beach, California.

Brian bootstrapped his way to success. In 1981, in talks and seminars around the U.S., he began teaching the principles he forged in sales and business. Today, his books and audio and video programs—more than 500 of them—are available in 38 languages and are used in 55 countries.

He is the bestselling author of more than fifty books, including *Full Engagement* and *Reinvention*.